MW01245684

Boo Boo Bunny
and Friends

THE COLOR OF FEELINGS

Written By
KAREN GALEHOUSE

Illustrated By
LISA WOHLWEND

Copyright © 2024 Karen Galehouse.

All rights reserved. This book or any portion thereof may not be reproduced
or used in any manner without the express written permission of the publisher
except for the use of brief quotations in a book review.

Published by Ingram Spark®, in the United States of America.
First printing, 2024.
ISBN: 979-8-218-23766-0

Text © 2024 by Karen Galehouse
Illustrations © 2024 by Lisa Wohlwend

www.karengalehouse.com

Dedicated to my brother John, who brought
happiness and love into so many lives.

"Class. Class." Mrs. Blatt says cheerfully.
"Yes. Yes." The class replies together.

"It's time to start our day.

I like how you are in a circle on the carpet so that
we can see and hear each other better as we learn.

This is our community circle."

"Let's look at this feelings poster. You can see BLUE, GREEN, YELLOW, and RED faces. There is a different emotion for each color. This poster will help us talk about our feelings."

"There are no 'good' or 'bad' feelings. Feelings are a part of us. They help us understand what is going on inside.

Let's see. Who can tell us a feeling?"

"Okay, Cinnie, what is your feeling word?"

"I am super excited this morning! I love all the things about school! My favorite things are books, pencils, markers, math, writing and the color blue!"

"Those are great things to be excited about, Cinnie.

On this poster YELLOW shows that you could feel silly, excited and a bit out of control.

Does anyone else ever feel silly, excited and a bit out of control?"

"Monk, why don't you tell us about a time that
you were excited?"

" I get excited all the time, but my most excited time
was on my birthday. We had banana cake with
banana ice cream. I turned **5** and my mom gave me
a puppy! He is white with black spots and I named him
Skip. He likes to run and play and be silly like me!"

"Being silly is fun, Monk. We can't wait to see pictures of Skip.

Who else would like to share a feeling?"

"Yes, Boo Boo. Tell us about a time when you felt happy."

"My family loves to go camping every summer. I get to sleep in a tent with my big brother and four sisters. We roast marshmallows over a campfire. Mine burns but I like to eat the crispy parts. Camping with my family makes me so happy."

"That sounds like an exciting adventure, Boo Boo!

Let's look at the poster again. It shows that 'happy' is the color GREEN.

In school, happiness can mean you feel calm, focused and ready to learn."

"Let's talk about one more feeling word before snack time."

"Hi. My name is Ping. This is my first day at school.
I think you are my teacher."

"Hi Ping. I am Mrs. Blatt. Welcome to our class.
We are talking about feelings."

"You can sit by me," Boo Boo Bunny offers. "I am a good helper. Ask me if you need help," Boo Boo Bunny adds. "Okay, thanks," Ping says nervously.

"That's Pinka." Boo Boo says to Ping.
"She gets mad a lot."

"Class. Class." Mrs. Blatt says.

"Yes. Yes." The class replies together.

"Who can tell me what emotion we just saw? Remember, emotions are important and they tell us something about ourselves."

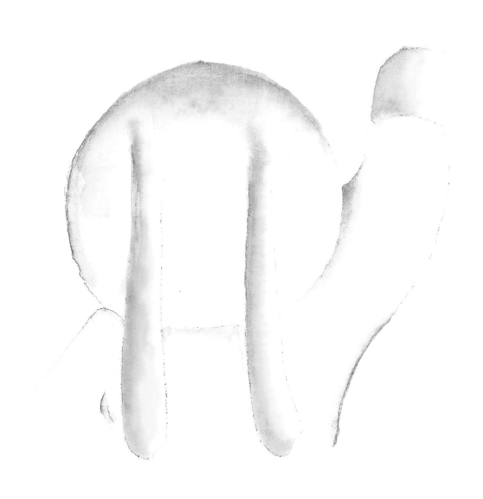

"That looks like a red one to me, Mrs. Blatt."

"You're right, Boo Boo. On this poster red shows that you can feel mad, mean, frustrated or your body feels out of control."

"It is okay to feel angry or frustrated but it is important to know what to do with all that angry energy. That is why we have our calming corner. Pinka made a good choice by drawing or coloring to calm herself."

"Mrs. Blatt, can I go sit with Pinka? She looks like
she would like a friend to color with her."

"Yes. Thank you for helping, Boo Boo."

"Next time in our community circle we will practice what to do when we have those red or angry feelings. You all did an amazing job sharing your feelings today."

"Now, it is time for a special snack that Ping brought to share with his new friends."

Visit **KarenGalehouse.com** or scan the QR code below to access downloads and more information.

Printed in the USA
CPSIA information can be obtained
at www.ICGtesting.com
CBHW060419041024
15321CB00015B/702